OCEAN JASPER

A Natural Wonder and a Geological Mystery

Susanne Lomatch

Susanne Lomatch
OceanJasper.org
http://www.oceanjasper.org

ISBN: 9781703393514

Table of Contents

Image Gallery

Hopefully these images will inspire you as much as they have me - they represent my dedication to understanding this amazing natural wonder of Planet Earth. More images available and updated at OceanJasper.org.

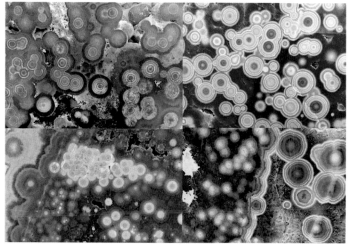

Colorful mix of banded/bullseye Ocean Jasper specimens

Colorful mix of "flower orb" Ocean Jasper specimens

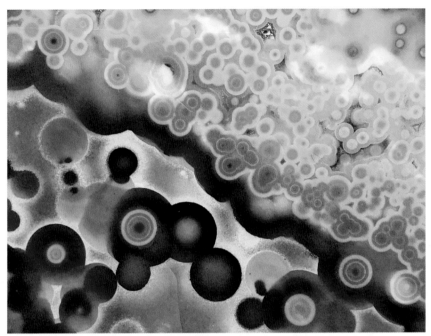

Beautiful macro photo of a closeup portion of a large high grade Ocean Jasper slab (translucent)

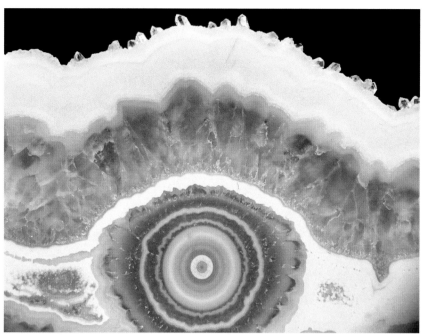

Beautiful macro photo of a closeup portion of a large high grade Ocean Jasper slab (large bullseye with over 20 rings, euhedral crystal shroud and terminated quartz edge)

High grade Ocean Jasper slab (bullseye) - Cover photo

Colorful faced rough Ocean Jasper specimen (translucent) – Front

Colorful faced rough Ocean Jasper specimen (translucent) - Side

Large high grade Ocean Jasper slab (ultra rare type with translucent vivid blues and large colorful bullseyes) - Front

Large high grade Ocean Jasper slab (ultra rare type with translucent vivid blues and large colorful bullseyes) - Back

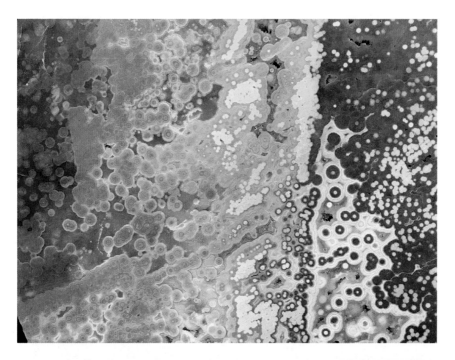

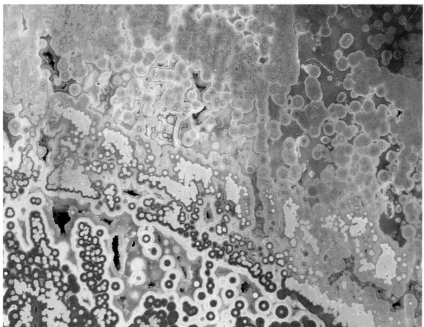

*Relief from an extra large Ocean Jasper slab (ultra rare hyper-
heterogeneous type with many pattern and color transitions)*

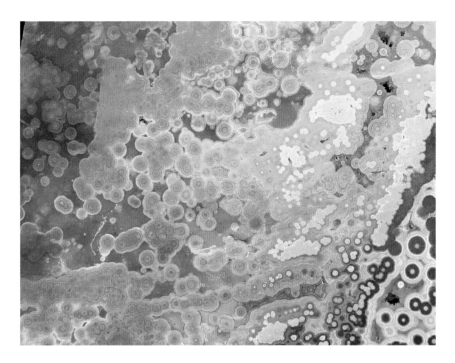

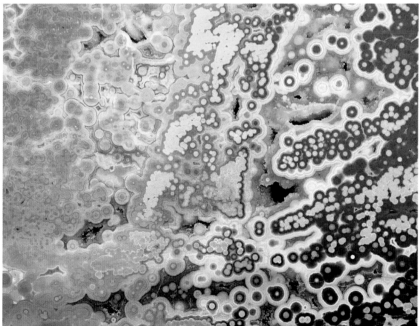

Relief from an extra large Ocean Jasper slab (ultra rare hyper-heterogeneous type with many pattern and color transitions)

Preface

Ocean Jasper (Spherulitic Chalcedony) is a natural large-scale formation wonder and a geological mystery. The true natural wonder of this unique and rare material from NW Madagascar region may never be known completely, since little or no cataloguing or classification of the original large-scale deposits at Marovato were undertaken. Much of the mined material has been taken out of Madagascar, sold and resold over the years, and processed, resulting in a loss of what may once have been a World Heritage site, if that truly could have been accomplished. It is this author's view that there should have been much more international attention given to this discovery in the early 2000s, to preserve the natural history of the deposits and to properly catalogue and understand how they were structured. This becomes evident to even the casual rock collector after viewing large format specimens from the Marovato deposits. The hyper-heterogeneous character of this material exhibits the widest variety of spherulitic orbicular structures, and a mind-blowing array of pattern and color variations, translucency and opacity transitions, and quartz crystal-chalcedony-botryoidal formations. It remains a geological mystery, with many missing technical details, such as host rock, age and compositional studies. I posit a speculative theory of formation based on existing information to whet the appetite of fellow researchers and enthusiasts.

One of the goals of this book is to promote the preservation of existing rare Ocean Jasper specimens, especially large-format slabs, faced-rough, rough, and polished displays showing the many amazing natural pattern and color variations. Another important goal of this book is to encourage comprehensive research studies, and I outline in detail a list of what is missing and needed.

All proceeds of this book will be donated to a research fund dedicated to furthering our understanding of this rare, mysterious and wonderful material, with the results of the studies available to the public domain.

A living public domain website is available at OceanJasper.org, where research papers and image galleries of specimens are updated as they are shared, either directly to the website or as a link to submissions on Mindat.org, the world's largest open database of minerals and rocks.

Finally, endowments of surviving large-scale specimens and other freeform specimens to mineral museums capable of long-term preservation, public display and researcher access are encouraged, both from collectors and lapidaries. The author's collection of rare slabs and specimens shown in this book are marked for such an endowment, as a commitment to conservation and preservation.

Susanne Lomatch
October, 2019

PART ONE
Ocean Jasper: Why We Need to Preserve It

Chapter 1
Historical Context

"Ocean Jasper" is a rare orbicular material found only in Madagascar (**Figure 1**). Its rarity however depends on grade quality and "vein type." Most orbicular materials, notably North American rhyolites and poppy jaspers, are for the most part homogenous materials, while rare-type Ocean Jasper is hyper-heterogenous. Ocean Jasper is also neither specifically a jasper nor an agate, but a "spherulitic chalcedony" [Lieber, 2003]. Indeed, mindat.org refers to "Ocean Jasper" as a "marketing term for a spherulitic variety of chalcedony." The name is an expired trademark filed in 2001 and held by one of the original distributors of the material to the North American market [The Gem Shop, 2019].

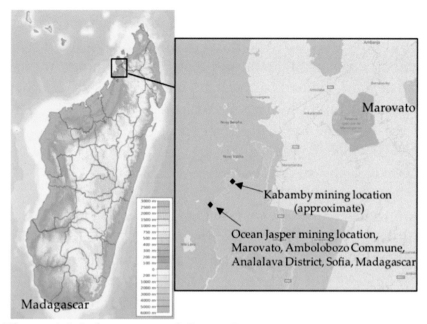

Figure 1. Madagascar and Ocean Jasper mining sites.

While some information on the deposits mined in Madagascar since 1999 has been published [Matthews, 2015], [The Gem Shop, 2019], little is known about the mining sites, such as detailed geological surveys. This information would certainly help researchers better understand the conditions that led to the creation of this unique material. In Part Two, I posit some "theories" on the genesis and evolution of this mineralogical wonder, based on available information.

Ocean Jasper has been long valued for its spherical orbs and colorful, mineral rich matrix. It has been a favorite of many lapidary cabochon cutters, and a significant amount of high-grade material mined has been cut into smaller size cabochons for jewelry settings or as collector cabs. The reported "rarity" of the material has driven the market prices up for raw material, and consequently the demand and prices for finished jewelry-sized cabochons.

Unfortunately, the demand and processing has resulted in a depletion of what may have once been available intact large-scale specimens of the material for study, and therefore a loss of information of what the mined deposits actually looked like, how they were structured, etc. It doesn't help that little and possibly no cataloguing and classification of the mined deposits were made during mining.

There are several possible reasons for a lack of cataloguing and classification of what was mined from 1999-2006. The mining industry was neglected by the government for decades prior to the mid-2000s [Wiki, Mining Industry of Madagascar]; it wasn't until 2005/6 that mining laws were enforced [Madagascar Mining Laws], increasing regulation on exports and strengthening claim permitting. The first two Ocean Jasper mines (or veins, as I will refer to them further) near Marovato were discovered by Paul Obeniche, a French gemstone dealer [Footnote 1]. These were Vein 1 (1996-2006) and Vein 2 (2005-2006), as identified in [Matthews, 2015]. The material from these veins is commonly referred to as "Old Stock" Ocean Jasper; for the sake of further discussion I subclassify "High Grade Old Stock" or "HGOS" as the highest grades from these veins.

The mining locations were documented as off the coast in a high tide area, however the mining veins were primarily located underground [Matthews, 2015], [The Gem Shop, 2019]. Mining techniques used were relatively rudimentary, as is the case with most gemstone mining in Madagascar, with local resident labor. This means hammers, picks, and dare I say it, jackhammers. Much of what was mined was taken by boat to a local port and warehouse, where chunks of rough material were further processed. Obeniche imported over a ton of material from Madagascar, including rough Ocean Jasper, to the Tucson Gem Show every year until the mines were depleted in 2006. In 2013, Obeniche transferred operations of his claims to Enter the Earth, a North Carolina company [Enter The Earth, 2019] that has since found two other significant deposits, Vein 3 (2013) and Vein 4 (2014) and a few other smaller pockets of material, all further inland from the original veins. Though all four veins have produced high grade material showing the best qualities of this unique spherulitic chalcedony, the highest grades and possibly the most important deposits are Vein 2 and "late" Vein 1, which produced large compound bullseye spherulites combined with translucent spherulites, all in a complex transition of patterns and color. I will provide numerous examples of this below; The cover photo of this book is of a beautiful large compound bullseye slab from Vein 2/late Vein 1, and **Figure 2** shows a large spectacular slab from Vein 1.

Figure 2. Large hyper-heterogeneous Ocean Jasper slab from Vein 1, approx. 8.5″ wide.

Another variety of Ocean Jasper, called "Kabamby," is still being mined near the original location, which is ~1.5 miles inland from the coast. This material has more similarities with North American poppy jaspers, especially from Morgan Hill, Pope Creek and Stony Creek, homogenous in variety in terms of patterns and colors. Kabamby material was discovered far before the more "exotic" varieties off the coast at Marovato. Indeed, a picture of a slab of it appears in the 1977 edition of The Illustrated Encyclopedia of Minerals & Rocks [Kourimsky, 1977]. A very similar set of specimens is shown in **Figure 3**, back-to-back slabs from Kabamby location; these are from the author's collection.

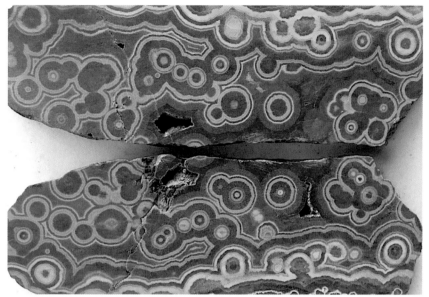

Figure 3. A set of slabs from Kabamby, similar to a specimen published in [Kourimsky, 1977], approx. 5″ length.

It isn't clear what the size range of the material mined was in the first two Marovato veins. We only have crude estimates [Matthews, 2015], [Enter The Earth, 2019] of this based on what information is available today, some 14 years later. Suffice it to say that large rough specimens were limited, and over time were processed down into much smaller specimen displays (e.g. spheres, palm stones, freeforms) or slabs, and then slabs cut into smaller cabochons for the jewelry and collector markets. Furthermore, though the types of material mined in Veins 1 & 2 were identified [Matthews, 2015], it isn't clear that these are accurate – information that I have gathered from lapidaries and other collectors suggest that either Vein 1 included more high-grade large bullseye/translucent material similar to that identified with Vein 2, or Vein 2 started producing material much earlier than noted in [Matthews, 2015] and in larger quantities than Vein 1. For example, the large polished slab shown in **Figure 2** was reportedly cut from a boulder chunk purchased in 2001 at Tucson [Terry Maple/ORCA, 2019], which would technically place it in the timeframe of Vein 1, not Vein 2 (see **Table 1**, Chapter 2). This ultra ultra high grade slab has large bullseye features combined with large flower orbs and translucent areas, and is a wonderful example of the hyper-heterogeneous character of this material.

Ocean Jasper is considered an "ornamental stone" in official reporting of mined material from Madagascar, as opposed to a gemstone, such as sapphire, ruby, tourmaline, etc. [USGS Minerals Yearbook, Madagascar]. Madagascar was a major producer of raw sapphires and rubies from 2000-2015, and has produced significant quantities of quartz and labradorite, also classified as ornamental stones. No official numbers are available of how much Ocean Jasper was mined from 1999-2015, as official quantities are buried in the ornamental stone category, which like all gemstone categories is underreported due to smuggled artisanal production and unregulated mining. Around 2004-5, the same timeframe as the mining code enactment, the Madagascan government reportedly required a portion of ornamental stones exported to be polished, such as faced rough freeform displays, spheres, palm stones, and slabs (see **Figure 4** for a few examples of polished display specimens imported from Madagascar), thereby strengthening the local lapidary trade and employment. This may have coincided with grants from the International Monetary Fund and the World Bank to build up Madagascar's mining industry [USGS Minerals Yearbook, Madagascar], to stave off economic collapse and unrest. Madagascar was and is a very poor country with a per capita GDP of ~USD$400-450 from 2002-2017. Over the same period there has been a boom-bust cycle of valuable gemstone and rock mining, affecting local economies and ecosystems [de Grave, 2017].

High grade Ocean Jasper is by far the most valuable and rare ornamental stone mined in Madagascar, and no new significant deposits of grades comparable to Vein 2/late Vein 1 have been discovered, though Veins 3 & 4 and a few isolated pockets have produced some beautiful material that also deserves motivation for preservation and further study.

Ocean Jasper Freeforms (Marovato)

Ocean Jasper Spheres (Marovato)

Ocean Jasper Cubes (Marovato)

Ocean Jasper Medallions (Kabamby)

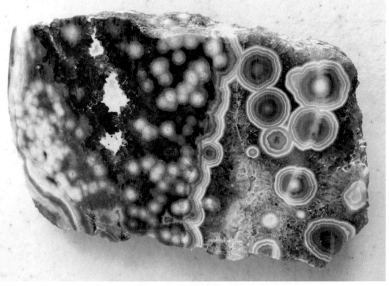

Ocean Jasper Faced Rough Slab (Marovato)

Ocean Jasper Translucent Slab (Marovato)

Figure 4. A few polished display specimens imported from Madagascar, mined in Marovato Veins 1 & 2 and Kabamby. More examples are found on OceanJasper.org.

Chapter 2
Size and Type Estimates of Mined Material

It is difficult to determine precisely the quantity and types of material mined at each location/vein. [Matthews, 2015] provides rough size estimates and show group pictures of particular material types mined from each major vein. Some scant information on what has been mined in the last 4 years is also available [Private Communication, C. Matthews, et al.]. These are compiled in **Table 1.**

Table 1: Mined Ocean Jasper Deposits		
Deposit/Vein	**Est. Size**	**Est. Location**
Marovato Vein 1 ("Old Stock"), 1999-2006	90x25 sqft, depth(s)/volume geometry not known	off the coast in tidal areas, underground
Marovato Vein 2 ("Old Stock"), 2005-2006	35x15 sqft, depth(s)/volume geometry not known	off the coast in tidal areas, underground
Marovato Vein 3, 2013	10x7 sqft, depth(s)/volume geometry not known	"further inland" from coast
Marovato Vein 4, 2014	Unknown	assume about the same as Vein 3
Kabamby, 2002-Present	15 sqmi surface collection	1.5 mi inland, location NE of Marovato
Ocean Wave, 2002-2006	Unknown	adjacent to Veins 1 & 2
New Finds/Pockets, 2015-2019 Group 1 Pocket (2015-2016) Group 2 Pocket (2017-2019)	Unknown; smaller "pockets" of material	Unknown; likely "further inland"

(Note 1: Sample photo of mined material for each deposit listed shown in the OceanJasper.org Gallery: http://www.oceanjasper.org/Gallery.html)
(Note 2: Ocean Wave - This material does not lack spherulites as commonly reported; I have several examples of this in my collection and from elsewhere.)

(Note 3: Group 1 Pocket - Produced some high grade/large irregular shaped bullseye material with colors and translucency, much of it sold into the Indian gemstone market for production of cabs and jewelry.)

(Note 4: Group 2 Pocket - Produced lower grade material with some defined orbicular and agate features, primarily green, beige in color. Some of this material was sold to China and appeared on the market in 2018; U.S. distribution premiered at the 2019 Tucson show, and sold in limited quantities to wholesalers at various shows.)

It is important to note that we have no exact data on the shape of the deposits, and importantly how deep they extended; the estimates for their area size in [Matthews, 2015] may be highly approximate. Therefore, we have no precise quantification of how much material was mined in each deposit in **Table 1**.

Large boulder size rough specimens of High Grade Old Stock (HGOS) Ocean Jasper were extracted from the Vein1 and Vein 2 deposits and sold on the open market [Footnote 2] in 2001 and later (and perhaps earlier, but I am basing the 2001 date on what was sold to a noted U.S. lapidary that specializes in slabbing large boulder specimens of material [Terry Maple/ORCA, 2019]). Some of these boulders were as large as 16"x12"x10" to 14"x10"x8" (>50lb) and produced a "family" of large and small slabs sold on the open market [Footnote 3]. Freeform displays as large as 12"x10" at the base, tapering to a height of 24" and polished spheres as large as 10-12" were sold to collectors, many of these displays cut and polished in Madagascar between 2003-2006, before export.

How large boulder chunks were situated or connected in the deposits is unknown, since no known cataloguing was done during the mining, 1999-2006. We do know that the material in these large boulders is contiguous spherulitic chalcedony without any host rock interspersed or surrounding the specimens. The boulder sizes were likely limited by the collection methods of local hand labor using hammers and picks, and the transport of boulders from the offshore underground mining location to shore using small boats.

In an attempt to quantify just how much HGOS material may have been mined in late Vein 1 and Vein 2, I have compiled data on HGOS slabs (which includes some faced rough) sold on eBay between 2006-2019. This data is compiled from archived sale information on WorthPoint, a collectible auction house repository source [Worthpoint, 2019], plus recent sale data on eBay itself. I include data on a few direct sales of HGOS collector slabs that I have purchased from slab lapidaries or other collectors. This data compilation is shown in **Table 2**. Note that this data does not include the many collector slabs/faced rough that have not resold on eBay, and even WorthPoint only provides a subset of what originally sold on eBay, though it is an extensive archive, and the only publicly available. So much rough, slabs and displays have been sold and resold over the years at yearly gem and mineral shows (such as Tucson) and that data is not available, nor do we know how much more HGOS was sold this way vs. eBay – we can only estimate from the WorthPoint/eBay data "sample."

In making this compilation effort, I classified various grade types of HGOS according to the scheme shown in **Table 3**. This grade classification is from my perspective as a collector, having seen thousands of specimens, from slabs/rough to polished displays to cabochons. I believe this classification will be helpful to other collectors and researchers. In addition to the grade classification scheme of **Table 3**, I also provide a classification of component features (basic archetypes) observed in HGOS Ocean Jasper material in **Table 4**.

Using the sample in **Table 2** we can further estimate the total cubic feet of material that may have produced the slabs/faced rough by making some volumetric assumptions of the source rough. Assuming 20% unique source rough for high grade and 5% for ultra high grade and above, and the following ellipsoidal volumetric forms of 4"x3"x2" (<=4"), 7"x5"x4" (5-7"), 10"x7"x6" (8-11"), 14"x10"x8" (>=12"), I obtain a total estimate of ~29677 cu-in. Making a further assumption that ~586 cu-in of material is ~50lb, this would imply a total source weight of ~2530lb. All of these assumptions on top of a sample to produce a total weight of material mined in Vein 1 and 2 is highly speculative, but it is a start. Obviously, the higher grades are rarer, with only ~5.5% of ultra ultra high grade slabs sold out of the total in the sample.

Table 2: Sample of HGOS OJ Slabs/FR Sold 2006-2019				
Grade	Size	Year sold	Count	Est Source Cu-In
High Grade	<=4"	2006-2019	805	2023
High Grade	5-7"	2006-2019	955	14001
High Grade	8-11"	2006-2019	146	6421
High Grade	>=12"	2006-2019	4	469
Ultra High Grade	<=4"	2006-2019	628	395
Ultra High Grade	5-7"	2006-2019	890	3262
Ultra High Grade	8-11"	2006-2019	152	1671
Ultra High Grade	>=12"	2006-2019	1	29
Ultra Ultra High Grade	<=4"	2006-2019	25	16
Ultra Ultra High Grade	5-7"	2006-2019	108	396
Ultra Ultra High Grade	8-11"	2006-2019	69	759
Ultra Ultra High Grade	>=12"	2006-2019	8	235
TOTAL			3791	29677

Table 3: Grade Classification Scheme for HGOS Ocean Jasper

Grade Class	Class Type	Comment
High Grade	Small Orb/Druzy	Small orb spherulitic chalcedony in a vuggy crystalline quartx druzy matrix. Semi-translucent.
High Grade	Small Orb/Opaque	
High Grade	Small Orb/Semi-Translucent	
High Grade	Large Orb/Opaque (Kabamby)	Only the finest slab specimens sold are included, and there were not many
High Grade	Large Orb/Semi-Translucent (Early Dig)	Large orbs are irregular, much less defined, no rings; many have small orb centers that may have rings
High Grade	Mixed Large-Small Orb not well defined/Opaque/Semi-Translucent	There are quite a few of these; the ultra HG is reserved for well-defined large orb material
High Grade	Small Orb/Translucent	
Ultra High Grade	<any of the above>	VIVID contrasted colors - these are rare and collectors covet them
Ultra High Grade	Large Orb/Druzy	Large orb spherulitic chalcedony in a vuggy crystalline quartx druzy matrix. May also contain small orbs. Semi-translucent.
Ultra High Grade	Large Orb/Opaque	
Ultra High Grade	Large Orb/Semi-Translucent	
Ultra High Grade	Large Orb/Translucent	
Ultra High Grade	Small Flower-burst Orb/Semi-Translucent	May contain druzy pockets
Ultra High Grade	Large Flower-burst Orb/Semi-Translucent	May contain druzy pockets
Ultra High Grade	Small Orb Transition Translucent-ST-Opaque-Druzy	Three or more transitions of types, small orbs, may also contain druzy, flower bursts
Ultra Ultra High Grade (Highest)	Large Orb Transition Translucent-ST-Opaque-Druzy	Three or more transitions of types, large orbs, may also contain small orbs, druzy, flower bursts

Table 4: Basic HGOS Ocean Jasper Archetypes	
Feature	**Archetypes**
Spherulitic Structure	"unbanded" banded/bullseye flower orb
Texture	chalcedony (clear or translucent) quartz (translucent) jasper (opaque))
Pattern	"homogenous" heterogenous hyper-heterogenous
Color	green, white, gray, cream, tan, brown, yellow, orange, pink, red, purple, blue, black <in order of occurrence: most to least likely>
Other Features	fortification patterns botryoids druzy pockets and edges euhedral or terminated quartz edges

(Note 1: Sample photos for each Archetype shown in the OceanJasper.org Gallery: http://www.oceanjasper.org/Gallery.html)

(Note 2: "Archetype" == An original model after which other similar things are patterned.)

(Note 3: There are quotes around "unbanded" – this is due to the fact that almost all Ocean Jasper orbs, even small, are banded, if one looks closely enough. Truly unbanded spherulites are the rarity.)

(Note 4: There are quotes around "homogeneous" – this is due to the fact that almost all Ocean Jasper is heterogenous, unlike other orbicular and poppy jaspers.)

Chapter 3
Geology of the Veins and Pockets

No geological surveys of the mined Ocean Jasper veins and pockets from **Table 1** are presently available in the public domain. The often-cited academic paper [Lieber, 2003] acknowledges that the deposits stretch "for several tens of square kilometers along the entire Analalava peninsula north of the provincial town of Mahajanga" and that "exact geological and mineralogical studies of the occurrence are missing." The reader should keep in mind that [Lieber, 2003] was written in 2003, and likely the quoted mining site area of 45x27 sq-m (148x89 sq-ft) referred to the area containing Vein 1 and Vein 2. The polished samples shown in [Lieber, 2003] are dated as mined mid-2003 or earlier, and include most major archetypes of Ocean Jasper in terms of spherulitic structure and texture, as described in **Table 4**.

It is my view that one cannot assume that the conditions and processes for each deposit occurrence in **Table 1** are the same, and therefore must be separated. Early Vein 1 material has more in common with some recently mined material found in inland pockets than late Vein 1 and Vein 2 material. Kabamby material shows some similarities with large bullseye orbicular material mined in late Vein 1 and Vein 2. Vein 1 and Vein 2 were discovered off the coast in a tidal area as underground deposits, and at least one of these veins extended inland from the beach. From [The Gem Shop, 2019]: "In 2006 the last rock from the deposit was mined. The deposit was followed from the beach into the side of the hill for about 40 meters. As the deposit was followed it became a large tube-like formation, extending straight into the host rock. The jasper deposit became thinner as work progressed. The mine is now depleted." It is not clear whether this reference was for Vein 1 or Vein 2, as both were reportedly mined to 2006 until depletion. The extension of the vein some 131 ft inland suggests that the shape of the first two veins were not regular (e.g. cubic), and that the estimates for their area size in [Matthews, 2015] may be highly approximate.

We have no exact data on the shape of the deposits, how deep they extended, the geology of the surrounding "host rock." Therefore, one is left to making some speculations, and with that, speculations on the conditions and processes of formation.

Chapter 4
Arguments for Preservation

I start with a few reasons why we need to preserve remaining large format "High Grade Old Stock" or "HGOS" Ocean Jasper material:

A. Rare in Large Forms (slabs, displays)
B. Loss of Information (pattern complexity; hyper-heterogeneity)
C. Loss of Natural History (natural art formations)

I address each of these aspects in detail.

A. Rare in Large Forms

Table 2 indicates just how rare large format material (> 8″) is compared to smaller formats: ~10% of the total resold through various sources from 2006-2019, with ultra ultra high grade (hyper-heterogenous) types the rarest (~2% of the total).

B. Loss of Information

Figure 5 shows an amazing array of hyper-heterogeneous slabs, with numerous transitions between near-clear chalcedony, translucent chalcedony, opaque chalcedony-jasper, and quartz, and with complex patterns and structural types of spherulites.

These surviving contiguous specimens are but a fraction of the contiguous varieties that were mined; some rare types are already lost due to processing for cabochons and smaller displays. What survives can be pieced together to form a rough map of what may have existed prior to removal from the mine. Keep in mind that the larger rough chunks were on the order of a cu-ft, and so a contiguous map can show spans of several cu-ft that may have existed before mining. It is a goal of this research project and preservation drive to complete such "cartographic maps" based on existing specimens, and from available photo archives of large format specimens that have been sold but may no longer be in existence (processed down for cabochons or small polished displays). Keep in mind that even though archival photos of large format specimens may exist, many are low resolution/poor quality and not sufficient for complete study. Therefore, this preservation drive stresses the need to preserve existing large format specimens, encourage reproduction of high resolution photos of specimens, and log them into an online mineral gallery, such as mindat.org, or submit them to oceanjasper.org where they will be catalogued and displayed with photographer/collector credit.

Figure 5. Slabs from U.S. lapidary "ORCA" showing a wonderful example of hyper-heterogeneous structure, with mining date est. c.2003 or earlier according to ORCA original purchase records from P. Obeniche. Largest slab is ~11.5" length. More slab and specimen examples are found on OceanJasper.org.

C. Loss of Natural History

I often find the artistic value of natural uncut slabs and faced rough more appealing than processed forms (smaller cabochons and polished freeform displays). Nature tends to produce "self-organized" art formations according to complex processes that no human artist can achieve. Buyers purchasing small cabochons often have no idea of the larger picture of natural art history they have procured a piece of. An archeological analogy is to take a rare large relief and cut it up into small pieces for the art or jewelry market – though this would be unpalatable to many in the archaeology realm, it has occurred over the years without question in the rare rock trade, driven by the lapidary and jewelry markets. It is most unfortunate that original cataloguing of the mined deposits of HGOS Ocean Jasper material was not undertaken. As explained previously, the reasons include mining with a profit motive in a poor country that had no requirement for stewardship of natural geological history. Of course, one can make that argument for many varieties of relatively rare rock that were and are mined and processed in rich first world countries, such as the U.S., so part of the problem is one of a lack of a stewardship culture for natural geological formations, a worldwide phenomenon that could change for the better. Collectors and researchers need to drive this cultural change. It won't entirely prevent cab lapidaries from cutting up rare material, but it can encourage more detailed photo cataloguing of what was and is mined and processed.

Chapter 5
Mine Deposit/Vein Reconstructions from Available Photo Archives – "Archetype Library"

Without documented classification and cataloguing of what was mined in Veins 1-4 and particularly Vein 2, we are left with the option of reconstructing "cartographic maps" of each vein from existing photo archives of specimens and cut cabochons, placing educated guesses on which vein each sample came from, and employing some sort of "intelligence" for reconstruction based on spherulitic structure, texture, pattern and color. Lower resolution photos can be processed with interpolation routines to increase size, useful for the many existing archived photos of rare specimens that are now "lost."

In addition to reconstructing "cartographic maps" as described, an "archetype library" of spherulitic structure, texture, pattern and color types can be assembled from archival photos. There are literally thousands of such archetypes in the Ocean Jasper material world – a highlight of just how hyper-heterogenous this material is compared to anything else in the petrographic world. Digital cloning techniques can be used to piece together smaller archetypes into what might have been a larger contiguous specimen. This is one goal of this site and research drive.

To start these efforts, a few photo samples of large specimens have been assembled into a set that might have represented a larger contiguous map, in **Figure 6**, and the beginnings of a much larger archetype library can be found in the OceanJasper.org Gallery: http://www.oceanjasper.org/Gallery.html.

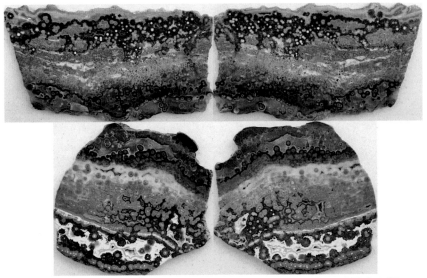

Figure 6. Front/back of two large slabs cut by ORCA/Terry Maple. Top slab is ~11″ length. More examples are found on OceanJasper.org.

Over time these cartographic maps and archetype library will grow with photo processing. A key to success of this project will come from other collectors, sharing photos of specimens that can be added. As such, this website provides a way for collectors to submit photos or links to photos/galleries of specimens in their collection here: http://www.oceanjasper.org/GallerySubmit.html. All submissions, photos or links, will be credited to the submitting collector/photographer.

Chapter 6
References & Footnotes (Part One)

References:

Lieber, W., "Spherulitic Chalcedony of Madagascar," Lapis, 28(9), p18-22, (2003). [In German; Translation by Susanne Lomatch available on the OceanJasper.org Research page: http://www.oceanjasper.org/Lieber2003.html]

Matthews, C., "The Geology, Varieties and History of Ocean Jasper, Part I," Enter the Earth Blog, January 2015. [http://www.entertheearth.com/the-geology-varieties-and-history-of-ocean-jasper-part-one]

The Gem Shop , "Ocean Jasper™" [https://thegemshop.com/pages/ocean-jasper]; also see the original 2001-2 trademark registration (now expired) here: http://tmsearch.uspto.gov/bin/showfield?f=doc&state=4804:x nkqwo.2.1]

Lomatch, S., "Ocean Jasper / Spherulitic Chalcedony of Madagascar: Model/Theory of Formation," (2019), available on the OceanJasper.org Research page: http://www.oceanjasper.org/Form_Final1.html]

Wikipedia,"Mining Industry of Madagascar" [https://en.wikipedia.org/wiki/Mining_industry_of_Madaga scar]

Madagascar Mining Laws (in French).
[http://edbm.mg/mining-laws-and-regulations/]

Enter the Earth (ETE) history on Etsy and Instagram pages, (2019).
[https://www.etsy.com/shop/EnterTheEarth?ref=simple-shop-header-name#about] and
https://www.instagram.com/entertheearth/?hl=en. On Instagram, ETE ran a series on the history that included more pictures and information than in [Matthews, 2015], link:
https://www.instagram.com/p/BuPAfARAGJx/.]

Kourimsky, J., "The Illustrated Encyclopedia of Minerals & Rocks," Chartwell Books, Inc., Figure 144, p. 136 (1977). The caption on the specimen photo: "Jasper - Camamba (Madagascar); 10cm."

USGS Minerals Yearbook, Madagascar.
[https://minerals.usgs.gov/minerals/pubs/country/africa.html#ma]

Terry Maple of MapleStuff/ORCA (eBay), a premier U.S. slab and rough lapidary that has cut collector grade Ocean Jasper slabs since 2001. Cited information from slab listings on eBay.

de Grave, A., "What happens after a mining rush? Photographs from Madagascar," Mongabay News, July 31, 2017. [https://news.mongabay.com/2017/07/what-happens-after-a-mining-rush-photographs-from-madagascar/]

Private Communication, Chris Matthews of ETE and a few gemstone dealers on eBay from India and China.

WorthPoint, (2019). [http://www.worthpoint.com]

Footnotes:

1. Paul Obeniche's name is sometimes shown as 'Obenich' in many original U.S. marketing documents and in other references.

2. The early open market for large rough chunks or boulders of Ocean Jasper primarily included the yearly Tucson gem and mineral show, with Paul Obeniche/Madagascar Minerals as one of the primary dealers. Some of these sales may have been wholesale or direct.

3. The open market for slabs from rough chunks includes online auction platforms like eBay, rock and mineral shows, and direct sales. Facebook and Instagram have also been selling platforms in recent years for slabs. The data I have compiled on slabs sold on eBay from 2006-2019 is from archived sale information on WorthPoint, a collectible auction house repository source, plus recent sale data on eBay itself.

PART TWO

Ocean Jasper (Spherulitic Chalcedony) of Madagascar: Model/Theory of Formation

Chapter 7
Key Distinguishing Features

Ocean Jasper is a Spherulitic Chalcedony with agate and jasper features. There have been many books and journal articles written about agate and jasper formation, and almost none written about Ocean Jasper, or Spherulitic Chalcedony, formation. Before presenting a new theory/model of formation, it is useful to highlight key distinguishing features of this amazing material.

The Primary Difference Between Ocean Jasper/Spherulitic Chalcedony and Conventional Agates

In Ocean Jasper, spherulitic chalcedony nucleates at "self-organized" points within in a large contiguous volume with size ranges that can span cu-ft, with microcrystalline fibers radiating outward in all directions from nucleation points. In conventional agates, spherulitic chalcedony nucleates at distinct points along a cavity wall, with typical agate cavities ranging from 6-15 cm in diameter, and microcrystalline fibers radiate toward the center of the vesicle. The attached diagrams help to elucidate this difference. **Figure 7** is a graphic of spherulite nucleation on the walls of a conventional agate vesicle with long fibrous microcrystalline chalcedony growth outward toward the center, opposing fibers meeting and forming common crystallization lines (adapted from [Moxon, 1996]). **Figure 8** shows a couple of slabs of Agua Nueva agate, sliced from nodules ranging in length from 13-15cm.

Figure 7. Graphic of spherulite nucleation on the vesicle walls of a conventional agate (adapted from [Moxon, 1996]).

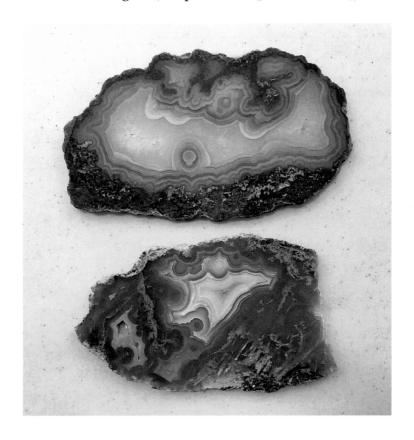

Figure 8. Agua Nueva agate slabs, sliced from nodules ranging in length from 13-15cm.

Figure 9 is a graphic of spherulite nucleation in Ocean Jasper, not along cavity walls but in a large three-dimensional open volume space occupied by the evolving precursor silica-rich fluid (see Chapter 9 for an explanation of this formation and evolution). The left image in **Figure 9** shows a "cell" of an evolved growth of three-dimensional banded spherulites with radial growth of long fiber microcrystalline chalcedony along lines that form the boundaries between spherulites. The resultant geometries of microcrystalline growth are polygonal shapes of varying sizes and orientations. This is an idealized model of what is observed visually in rough Ocean Jasper specimens (e.g. **Figure 10**), and also in polarized light microphotography, such as shown here: http://www.alexstrekeisen.it/immagini/meta/oceanjasper(25).jpg [Strekeisen]. As stated by [Vernon, 1996], "A dark 'extinction cross' is common in spherulites observed in crossed polars, because many fibers (each with one of the principal optical vibration directions parallel to its length) are parallel or approximately parallel to the vibration direction of the polarizer and analyzer, no matter what the orientation of the spherulite."

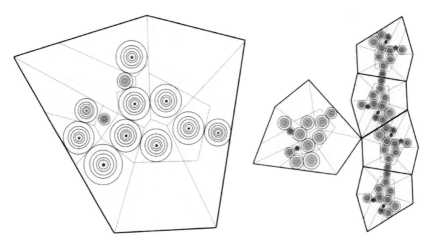

Figure 9. Graphic of spherulite nucleation in Ocean Jasper/Spherulitic Chalcedony. **Left:** Idealized "cell" of banded spherulites, with boundaries/growth interference between spherulites forming irregular polygonal geometries. **Right:** More complex heterogenous generalization of the basic cell structure that one might see in Ocean Jasper specimens.

Figure 10. Faced rough Ocean Jasper specimen from Kabamby showing irregular polygonal boundaries/shapes where spherulites meet. Specimen is ~ 12cm length. Front (top); back (bottom).

The Primary Difference Between Ocean Jasper/Spherulitic Chalcedony and Conventional Orbicular Jaspers

In Ocean Jasper, spherulitic structure and pattern formation is heterogeneous to hyper-heterogeneous. In conventional orbicular jaspers, spherulitic structure and patterns are more homogeneous. The right image in **Figure 9** is a graphic of a more complex heterogenous generalization of the basic cell structure that one might see in Ocean Jasper specimens. **Figure 11** shows a more homogeneous generalization of typical patterns in conventional orbicular jaspers. Pictures of the attached specimen samples help to elucidate this difference: **Figure 12** is a hyper-heterogenous specimen of Ocean Jasper, a large old stock slab spanning over 11" showing numerous transitions between transparent chalcedony layers, translucent chalcedony layers, and chalcedony-quartz layers, each with numerous heterogenous spherulite patterns of widely differing structure. **Figure 13** is a more homogenous specimen of orbicular jasper from China. **Figure 14** displays a single photo of all specimens, Agua Nueva, Ocean Jasper and Orbicular Jasper from China to show the range in sizes and complexity.

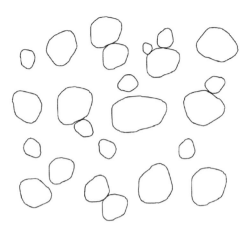

Figure 11. Graphic of homogeneous generalization of typical patterns in conventional orbicular jaspers.

Figure 12. Large slab specimen of high-grade old stock Ocean Jasper from Marovato showing hyper-heterogenous patterns and layers. Specimen is ~ 11.5″ length.

Figure 13. Orbicular jasper from China, showing a more homogeneous pattern arrangement. Specimen is ~ 15cm length.

Figure 14. Comparison photo of slab specimens: Agua Nueva, Ocean Jasper, Orbicular Jasper from China.

The Primary Difference Between Ocean Jasper/Spherulitic Chalcedony and Dendritic/Plume Agates

This difference is simple: there are almost [Footnote 4] no observed dendritic features in Ocean Jasper, unlike those seen in dendritic agates or conventional agates with dendritic features, and there are very few instances of plume-like features, as observed in plume agates. This difference is important, since the nucleation and growth of spherulites and the growth of dendrites and plumes follow a distinctly different set of conditions [Vernon, 1996], which will help aid a complete theory/model of formation. Spherulites are aggregates of separate crystals, contrasted with dendrites, which are branched single crystals. The aggregates are radiating arrays of fibrous (needle-like, acicular) crystals, where each fiber has the same crystallographic axis parallel to its length, and each has an orientation slightly different from that of its neighbors.

As stated by [Vernon, 1996], "Spherulites form under conditions of very strong supersaturation. The reason for the development of spherulites, rather than dendrites, is that the diffusion rate (D) is even lower than for dendritic growth, as expected for glasses and viscous silicate melts. In spherulitic growth, an extremely narrow 'impurity' layer of thickness ∂ = D/G (commonly less than 10^{-4} cm wide) develops around the very slowly growing crystal. The result is that minute projections on the nucleus grow into new crystals and furthermore, that very small projections on the fibers themselves can develop into new fibers."

Other Unique Features of Ocean Jasper/Spherulitic Chalcedony: Quartz Pseudomorphs

An often-observed progression of spherulitic growth and banding are crystalline quartz outgrowths surrounding each spherulite, commonly known as "flower orbs." A graphic is shown in **Figure 15**. This modality/habit can be considered pseudomorphic in the sense that it appears in an atypical form contrasted with the aggregate structure on which it appears – one polymorph habit replacing another. Even more interesting is observed agate-like banding that can occur enveloping each "flower orb." A spectacular example of this is shown in the pictured specimen in **Figure 16**, where cross-sections of large flower orbs with such "shroud-banding" can be seen floating in near clear chalcedony. Though this specimen is of a rare translucent variety, large "cogwheel" flower orbs appear in more opaque specimens such as those featured in **Figure 12**. The flower orb/cogwheel is somewhat unique in the petrographic world, and specimens that feature them are rated ultra-high grade.

Figure 15. Graphic of "flower orb" spherulite structure with pseudomorphic quartz "petals." The right graphic shows a subset of these possible modalities with an agate-like banded outer ring.

Figure 16. Polished freeform Ocean Jasper specimen showing "flower-orbs" floating in translucent/near clear chalcedony. Note each compound spherulite has a center with translucent pseudomorph quartz outgrowths, surrounded by banded rings of chalcedony. The cross-section allows us to see the 3D shroud of chalcedony around each spherulite structure.

Chapter 8
Existing Theory of Formation and Issues/Critiques

From Campos-Venuti: "Ocean Jasper is an orbicular jasper formed from devitrification of an obsidian lava flow and forms the typical devitrification spherulites. The process continues and a jasper with an orbicular structure ultimately is formed. At this stage, the spherulites are not yet banded. The disequilibrium of the jasper causes its softening in a colloidal phase, and during this stage the spherulites grow with bands of both chalcedony and quartz depending on the degree of dilution. At this point in certain areas of the deposit there is recrystallization of the transparent chalcedony. In other areas, we have a return to the stability of the jasper with the formation of those wonderful replacements of jasper on quartz spherulites, also famous in Morgan Hill Poppy Jasper from California." [Campos-Venuti, 2018]

Campos-Venuti bases the evolution of Ocean Jasper from devitrified obsidian to all of its present forms on a multi-phase process that primarily involves repeated changes in groundwater chemistry, dilution from an alkali-silica reaction, recrystallization, etc. of silica polymer colloids originating from obsidian.

I don't reject this view of Ocean Jasper formation, but it suffers from several problems:

1. There is little published evidence that the geology of the surrounding host rock is rhyolitic/obsidian. Obsidian is found in locations which have experienced rhyolitic (extrusive) eruptions. Madagascar does not have any significant notable history of such volcanic activity, instead the entire island is of mixed origin spanning many geological epochs and types of rock formation, and the entire island is separated by a shear zone running NW-SE that possibly separates two different crustal terrains [Ashwal & Tucker, 1999]. The northwestern coastal inland area does contain sparse deposits of volcanic rock from the Tertiary and Quaternary, but is otherwise largely of recent sedimentary formation ("The western third is composed of two large basins of late Paleozoic to recent sedimentary and volcanic rocks (Morondava and Mahajanga basins)." [Ashwal & Tucker, 1999]).

2. Spherulitic nucleation can occur in numerous ways, not just from devitrification of volcanic glasses, but also from supercooled silica melt [Vernon, 1996]. It is not evident that devitrification is the source of spherulitic nucleation in Ocean Jasper and that volcanic glass (e.g. obsidian) is source of high silica content material that eventually formed silica polymer colloids that then formed chalcedony, jasper and quartz layers.

3. The evolved Ocean Jasper deposits are large contiguous heterogeneous arrays of spherulites with widely differing chalcedony, jasper and quartz content, and with wide variation in spherulitic forms. Though the groundwater/dilution theory is interesting and plausible, there is no solid evidence that this is the cause of the large-scale heterogeneous deposits that have been found.

Chapter 9
Proposed Theory/Model of Formation

The attached diagram (**Figure 17**) depicts a proposed theory/model of formation of Ocean Jasper/Spherulitic Chalcedony. The model starts with a large volume cavity, on the order of cu-ft or several cu-ft, filled with a silica-rich fluid composed of water, silica and impurities that is completely or partially in solution. Though it is uncertain what the host rock is for the large cavity, this model assumes it to be intrusive granitic with intense pressure and temperature variations from magmatic processes. The cavity filled with a silica-rich fluid undergoes a supercooled phase leading to supersaturation and spherulitic nucleation at "self-organized" points in the fluid solution. At each nucleation point a nanometer-sized crystallite (grain) of silica precipitates out of solution and becomes a growth center for a larger three-dimensional spherulite. As time progresses the solution becomes increasingly supersaturated, but the water content is still high, with silica precipitates polymerizing and fibrous crystal growth occurring radially in all directions from nucleation points. Banding of developing spherulites occurs as a result of repeated polymerization amidst repeated radial fibrous crystal growth, with color provided by mineral impurities (e.g. iron oxides) that are distributed within the spherical layers of the spherulite. Surrounding each developing spherulite is a silica solution that continues to undergo the supersaturation/precipitation/polymerization cycle as the silica/water content increases, eventually leading to a colloidal mixture of insoluble structures (developing spherulites and silica precipitates that polymerize) in the remaining silica solution. Depending on the level of initial impurities, the local character of the colloid can be either a gel or a sol. As the water content reduces, the entire spherulite colloidal matrix starts to crystallize/harden into chalcedony, crystalline quartz or jasper, with agate-like fortifications forming between contracting areas and pure crystalline quartz growth occurring in cavities (druzy). Whether the colloidal gel matrix crystallizes into chalcedony or crystalline quartz depends on the degree of bound water held within the silicon dioxide: hydrous vs. anhydrous.

An elaborated note about how spherulite banding occurs in this model. The repeated banding is particularly a result of precipitation of silica and the formation of ring patterns from precipitates. As mentioned above, these occur amidst polymerization of precipitates and radial fibrous crystal growth. Such rings or bands are Liesegang type precipitation patterns that are replete in other chemical systems undergoing a precipitation reaction under certain conditions of concentration and in the absence of convection. There is specific support for this dynamic in the literature [Polezhaev & Müller, 1994]. See also [Wiki, Liesegang Rings].

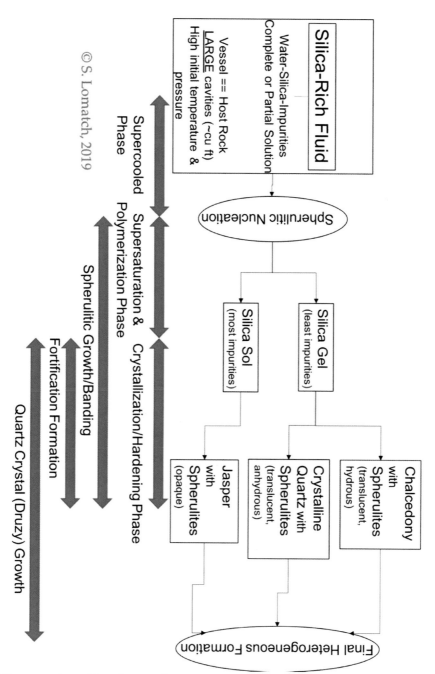

Figure 17. Graphic of proposed theory/model of Ocean Jasper/Spherulitic Chalcedony formation.

The amazing hyper-heterogenous specimen shown in **Figure 12** shows chalcedony, quartz and jasper "layers" with a wide variety of spherulites in terms of composition and complexity.

It is important to note that this model features self-organizational nucleation and crystallization, and the resultant uniquely large-scale complex heterogenous spherulitic patterns that are developed and observed are likely from dynamic reaction-transport type interactions ([Ortoleva, et al., 1987], [Heaney & Davis, 1995]), not from arrangement or alignment according to original layering of a lava flow [Campos-Venuti, 2012, 2018]. Though I have left out many details of this nonlinear dynamic formation process, there is a whole field of research to support it, including formalisms and mathematical modeling techniques ([Nicolis & Prigogine, 1977], [Ortoleva, et al., 1987], [Epstein & Pojman, 2006]).

Future research can include further development of the above outlined model, including more details on the unknowns/initial conditions (see list below) and possibly even a simulation based on a mathematical model to show the various pattern formations that are observed.

Pros:

This model supports the observed existence of near spherical three-dimensional spherulites, usually multiply banded (rings). These "perfect" structures are rarely observed anywhere else in the petrographic world. A model such as this one where nucleated spherulites grow suspended in a silica solution turned colloid mixture is both physically and chemically plausible. This is the first kind of such a model for this unique material.

Differentiators:

This model does not rely on periodically changing outside causes, such as groundwater infiltration or changes in groundwater chemistry or on an alkali-silica reaction ("concrete cancer") or on alignment to lava flows to explain formation.

Chapter 10
Missing Information and Future Research Studies

The following is a concise list of incomplete information and data, prompting future research studies as outlined.

-**Host Rock** [Geological Surveys]
-**Age** [Dating Studies]
-**Complete mineralogical/chemical/crystallographic "blueprint"** [Compositional Studies]
-**Initial temperature and pressure of silica-rich fluid precursor** [Modeling/Simulations]
-**Development/formation time of material** [Modeling/Simulations]

Host Rock:

The identification of the host rock(s) of Ocean Jasper/Spherulitic Chalcedony specimens remain unknown. It is widely reported that Ocean Jasper is "silicified rhyolite" and that the discovered "veins" near Marovato were in large tube-like formations within the host rock that extended from off-shore (under water during high tide) to the beach and inland – see Part One for original references to this.

No geological surveys or compositional studies of the host rock(s) surrounding the mined Marovato veins are publicly available. Though Kabamby Ocean Jasper specimens were reportedly collected near the inland surface, it is also unknown what the surrounding host rock composition is in that collection area, which spans several square miles.

It seems plausible that the host rock is rhyolite from extrusive lava flows, until one considers just how large the formations actually are – contiguous cu-ft in several directions without any break. Though cataloguing of the mined deposits was not completed (at least not available publicly), the contiguous scale of the deposits can be clearly seen from the many slab specimens of large boulder-sized chunks of the material.

The "chamber" in which the original silica-rich fluid started to form spherulitic chalcedony may have been very large and quite solid, providing significant initial pressure and temperature. A surface chamber of volcanic rhyolite seems less likely given the parameters of the discovered deposits.

Intrusive granite, which is very high in silica content (73%), may have been a candidate for the host chamber, providing the necessary initial conditions for the silica-rich fluid, pressure and temperature. If that were the case, then development time for the deposits may have spanned a significantly long time, and may explain the scale and complexity observed in the material. Though the deposits were found at or near the surface, their birth location may have been much deeper underground, and as Madagascar evolved to its present-day location, the deposits "uplifted" through a significant commensurate period of upheaval of the earth's crust with the migration of Madagascar itself.

A complete geological survey of the mined areas and any of the host rocks needs to be completed for clear assessment.

Age:

Dating rocks with no organic material and variable/unknown exposure to the surface is difficult. Absolute dating techniques such as radiocarbon dating and cosmogenic nuclide dating are useful for organic-based fossils and rocks that have consistently had surface exposure for the duration of their existence. Cosmogenic nuclide dating can be done but may be indeterminate if the material formed deeper underground and over time shifted to the surface. Some materials are better suited for this type of dating - granite and other rocks with large amounts of crystalline quartz may contain cosmogenic nuclides (e.g. Berillium-10) trapped in the quartz crystal lattice following spallation reactions with incident cosmic ray neutrons. This dating technique is worth pursuing even though there may be some indeterminate result due to shifting depth of the material over its duration of life. A disadvantage is that the technique is completely destructive – a sample of the material is crushed and repeatedly exposed to Hexafluorosilicic acid until Beryllium Oxide powder precipitates out and is analyzed by an accelerator mass spectrometer to calculate the ratio of Be-10 to naturally occurring isotopes. There are numerous research labs at universities and companies that can perform this test on a few samples.

Other techniques include luminescence dating, which measures the accumulation of electrons trapped in imperfections in the crystal structure of the material as a result of exposure to radioactive isotopes and their ionizing radiation. Two limiting factors of this technique are the requirement that the material undergo somewhat constant exposure to the radioisotopes over the duration of life, and that electron traps in the crystal structure are limited over time.

Relative dating techniques can also be done by completing a geological survey of the mined deposits and the surrounding host rocks, as above. This can include paleomagnetic/magnetostratigraphy dating methods.

Due to the uncertainty of the birth location of the mined material, precise age from dating techniques may not be possible. Cosmogenic nuclide dating should be done anyway on several small samples with significant crystalline quartz content.

Compositional Studies:

Thorough compositional studies of Ocean Jasper/Spherulitic Chalcedony have not been completed. The makeup is largely silica polymorphs (e.g. chalcedony, quartz) and trace minerals (e.g. iron oxides) that provide color. A complete "blueprint" of all polymorph and mineral content is scientifically useful for understanding formation, especially of a complex specimen such as that shown in **Figure 12**.

In particular, attention to a detailed map of spherulite microstructure amidst surrounding chalcedony/quartz matrix is desirable, identifying all mineral impurities that are included. Applicable techniques are laser-interference microscopy (detects small differences in refractive index), transmission and scanning electron microscopy (measuring detailed microstructure, 3D surface morphology, compositional zoning), and X-ray compositional mapping using several methods of spectrometry. There are numerous research labs at universities and companies that can perform these studies on a few key specimens.

A complete compositional study of key specimens needs to be completed for clear assessment.

Modeling/Simulation Studies:

Modeling and simulation studies have been done on agates and chalcedony, from an experimental perspective [Moxon, 1996] and from a numeric computational perspective [Wang & Merino, 1990], [Ortoleva, et al., 1987]. There also exists a wide body of theoretical and modeling research on spherulitic nucleation and growth, [Gránásy, et al., 2005] and references therein. These efforts will form a basis for future modeling and simulation studies of Ocean Jasper/Spherulitic Chalcedony.

Important unknown variables include content of silica-rich fluid precursor, initial pressure/temperature, viscosity of fluid during formation, degree of supercooling and supersaturation, duration of formation time. Important dynamics include spherulitic nucleation and growth, reaction-diffusion, hydrodynamics (and possibly hydrothermal activity), polymer chemistry and crystallization.

Modeling/Simulation studies can provide some indication of how this material formed, even though many geological unknowns exist. Compositional studies should be done commensurately to form a complete theory/model.

Chapter 11
References & Footnotes (Part Two)

References:

Ashwal & Tucker, "Geology of Madagascar: A Brief Outline," Gondwana Research, v.2 (3) p335-339, (1999).

Campos-Venuti, "Genesis and Classification of Agates and Jaspers: A New Theory," Tipografia Luciani, (2012).

Campos-Venuti, "Banded Agates: A Genetic Approach," Edizioni AccorpaMente, (2018).

Epstein & Pojman, "Introduction: Self-organization in nonequilibrium chemical systems," Chaos, v.16, (2006).

Gránásy, Pusztai, Tegze, Warren, and Douglas, "Growth and Form of Spherulites," Physical Review E, v.72 (1) p011605, (2005).

Heaney & Davis, "Observation and Origin of Self-Organized Textures in Agates," Science, v.269, p1562-1565, (1995).

Moxon, "Agate Microstructure and Possible Origin," Terra Publications, (1996).

Nicolis & Prigogine, "Self-Organization in Nonequilibrium Systems," Wiley, New York, (1977).

Polezhaev & Müller, "Complexity of precipitation patterns: Comparison of simulation with experiment," Chaos, v.4, p631, (1994).

Ortoleva, Merino, Moore & Chadam, "Geochemical self-organization I; reaction-transport feedbacks and modeling approach," American Journal of Science, v.287, p979-1007, (1987).

Strekeisen, See website
http://www.alexstrekeisen.it/english/meta/oceanjasper.php
for numerous polarized light microphotographs of Ocean Jasper samples showing spherulites and fibrous chalcedony with irregular polygon boundaries. Cited example:
http://www.alexstrekeisen.it/immagini/meta/oceanjasper(25).jpg.

Vernon, "A Practical Guide to Rock Microstructure," Cambridge University Press, (1996).

Wang & Merino, "Self-organizational origin of agates: Banding, fiber twisting, composition, and dynamic crystallization model," Geochimica et Cosmochimica Acta v.54 (6) p1627-1638, (1990).

Wikipedia, "Liesegang Rings"
[https://en.wikipedia.org/wiki/Liesegang_rings]

Footnotes:

4. Leo Jahaan brought to my attention two specimens in his extensive collection showing dendritic features, outward radial growth of dendrites in a spherulite in one specimen, and as inclusions in another specimen. It is unclear where or when these specimens were mined, neither appear to be from the original two Marovato veins. This may indicate the importance for subclassification of Ocean Jasper based on mining location.

Glossary

Entries are listed according to the logical flow of concepts discussed in this book.

Silica: The term silica generally covers all of the polymorphs of silicon dioxide (SiO_2). These polymorphs include pure silica polymorphs that are made up of SiO_4 tetrahedra, quartz (triagonal), moganite (monoclinic), tridymite (triclinic), cristobalite (tetragonal), keatite, coesite and silica glass, but also silica polymorphs that are intergrowths of these, such as chalcedony, and contain impurities such as opal and jasper. "Druzy" quartz is crystalline quartz with repeating triagonal structure.

Chalcedony: Chalcedony is microcrystalline quartz (SiO_2) formed from a silica-rich fluid. Agate and jasper are both varieties of chalcedony, as is carnelian, chrysoprase and onyx. Chalcedony is a hard material (Mohs scale 6.5-7), has a very smooth, non-granular texture, conchoidal fracture and a waxy to vitreous luster, and a semi-transparent to translucent diaphaneity. Structurally, chalcedony is composed of aggregates of micron and submicron fibrous (parallelly-grown) quartz crystals [1] and has also been found to be very fine intergrowths of quartz and moganite [2]. Mindat [1] defines two types of chalcedony, length-fast and length-slow, distinguished between how each crystallite (grain) is oriented relative to the c-axis (parallel or perpendicular). Chalcedony is more soluble than quartz under low-temperature conditions due to its ultrafine grain and moganite content. Chalcedony tends to develop radially grown "fibers", resulting in botryoid (grape shaped), round and stalactite habits. Often seen is concentric banding perpendicular to the fiber orientation (e.g. in agates).

[1] See Refs on Mindat: https://www.mindat.org/min-960.html.

[2] Heaney, Peter J. (1994). "Structure and Chemistry of the low-pressure silica polymorphs". In Heaney, P. J.; Prewitt, C. T.; Gibbs, G. V. (eds.). Silica: Physical Behavior, geochemistry and materials applications. Reviews in Mineralogy. 29. pp. 1–40.

Agate: An agate is a translucent to semitransparent chalcedony, generally with banding, but there are named agates without obvious bands that are translucent with plume-shaped, dendritic or mossy inclusions. Indeed, the non-banded agates might be better called "included chalcedony" or specifically, "mossy chalcedony" "dendritic chalcedony" or "plume chalcedony." Agates form in both igneous and sedimentary rocks, with much rarer formation in metamorphic and plutonic rocks. Agate formation can occur in hollow cavities (nodules) or cracks and fractures (veins).

Jasper: A jasper is an opaque chalcedony, more precisely, a chalcedony with impurities that reduce the material from semitransparent or semitranslucent to opaque. This is a strict definition of a jasper. It is important to note that "jasper" is also a loosely applied term in common usage to describe many types of rock, even those that may not even be a jasper (e.g. Bumblebee Jasper from Indonesia).

Orbicular Jasper: According to Mindat.org: "a name given to a highly silicified rhyolite or tuff that has quartz and feldspar crystallized into radial aggregates of needle-like crystals forming orbicular (spherical) structures." It is important to note that this definition is a restricted one of a subset of material that falls under a more general class of material with orbicular structures, "Orbicular Rock". That general class includes Spherulitic Chalcedony ("Ocean Jasper"), along with many other types of material with orbicular structures, some of which may not have originated from "highly silicified rhyolite or tuff".

Orbicular Rock: A general class of rock material with orbicular structures. Includes orbicular rhyolites and Spherulitic Chalcedony. Orbicular rhyolites tend to be more homogeneous in orbicular pattern, with structures that are far from spherical (e.g. highly oblate and irregular). Spherulitic Chalcedony is heterogeneous in orbicular pattern, with banded spherical structures.

Rhyolite: An igneous, extrusive volcanic rock ("volcanic"), of felsic composition (relatively rich in elements that form quartz and feldspar, both silicate minerals). It may have any texture from glassy to fine grained to larger grained. It is the extrusive equivalent to granite, meaning rhyolite forms as magma expels and cools above the surface of the Earth's crust.

Granite: An igneous, intrusive volcanic rock ("plutonic"), of felsic composition that is granular with coarse-grained texture and larger-scale crystal structure. Granite forms within Earth's crust from the cooling and crystallization of magma.

Spherulites: Spherulites are spherical and spheroidal structures that develop from radial fibrous crystal growth from nucleation points. Spherulites are aggregates of separate crystals, contrasted with dendrites, which are branched single crystals. The aggregates are radiating arrays of fibrous (needle-like, acicular) crystals, where each fiber has the same crystallographic axis parallel to its length, and each has an orientation slightly different from that of its neighbors. Spherulites can form in volcanic glasses (devitrification in obsidian) and in supercooled silica melts. Spherulites can be banded or singular (no banding).

Spherulitic Chalcedony: Also known under the marketing name "Ocean Jasper". Neither specifically a jasper nor an agate, this rare material is a heterogeneous mix of spherulites in a translucent chalcedony, semi-translucent crystalline quartz and opaque jasper matrix, exhibiting complex transitions between each, and a wide variety colors and patterns on a large scale compared to a conventional agate or jasper.

Nucleation: The first step in the formation of either a new thermodynamic phase or a new structure via self-assembly or self-organization. Nucleation is often found to be very sensitive to impurities in the system.

Supersaturation: A solution that contains more of the dissolved material than could be dissolved by the solvent under normal circumstances. Special conditions need to be met in order to generate a supersaturated solution – one of them is temperature dependence of solubility. If a solution were to be suddenly cooled (supercooled) at a rate faster than the rate of precipitation, the solution will become supersaturated until the solute precipitates to the temperature-determined saturation point. The precipitation or crystallization of the solute takes longer than the actual cooling time because the molecules need to meet up and form the precipitate without being knocked apart by water. Thus, the larger the molecule, the longer the solute will take to crystallize due to the principles of Brownian motion. Supersaturated solutions can undergo nucleation, such as spherulitic crystal growth, under certain conditions. Crystallization will occur to allow the solution to reach a lower energy state. A crystallization phase diagram shows where undersaturation, saturation, and supersaturation occur at certain concentrations.

Liesegang Rings/Patterns: Liesegang rings and patterns are a phenomenon seen in many, if not most, chemical systems undergoing a precipitation reaction under certain conditions of concentration and in the absence of convection. Liesegang pattern formations have been observed in chemical, physical, biological and geological systems. A few specific examples: Silver-chromate precipitate pattern in a layer of gelatin, colored bands of cement observed in sedimentary rocks, banding in agates, and the banding/rings in spherulites of Ocean Jasper (Spherulitic Chalcedony).

Polymer: A polymer is a large molecule, or macromolecule, composed of many repeated subunits, created via polymerization of many small molecules, known as monomers.

Colloid: A mixture in which one substance of microscopically dispersed insoluble particles is suspended throughout another substance. Since this is not a homogenous mixture it is NOT a solution. [So "colloidal solution" is a misnomer.] A colloid is a heterogeneous mixture. Sometimes the dispersed substance alone is called the colloid; the term colloidal suspension refers unambiguously to the overall mixture. Unlike a solution, whose solute and solvent constitute only one phase, a colloid has a dispersed phase (the suspended particles) and a continuous phase (the medium of suspension). To qualify as a colloid, the mixture must be one that does not settle or would take a very long time to settle appreciably.

Colloidal Silica: Colloidal silica is formed from the polymerization of small dissolved silica molecules into larger colloidal particles by precipitation, condensation, or redox reactions. The first step in this process is the neutralization of the silica solution, leading to the formation of nanometer size silica nuclei, or subunits of colloidal silica particles. How these subunits are joined together to form larger polymerized colloidal particles and colloid suspensions (gel or sol) depends on the conditions of polymerization.

Sol: A sol is a colloid made out of very small solid particles dispersed in a continuous liquid medium. Example: mud.

Gel: A gel is a colloid made out of molecules of a liquid dispersed within a solid. Example: jelly.

Homogeneous: Uniform in composition or character.

Heterogeneous: Distinctly nonuniform and diverse in composition or character.

About the Author

I have a research background in physics and engineering. I started collecting "Ocean Jasper" almost 5 years ago, first buying cabochons, then focusing on larger polished medallion and display or "palm stone" specimens, until these were not available in the quality of what some term high grade "old stock" material. I continued to buy collector grade cabochons, and in early 2018, I realized that I should have been buying collector grade slabs and high quality rough during those 5 years. I decided at the same time that there simply isn't enough research out there on this material, and that not enough preservation of large-scale specimens was being done so that future researchers and mineral enthusiasts could study this amazing (and now depleted) material. I am presently working to build a collection for complete research study, and to encourage others to support preservation and study of this material over further processing loss.

Made in the USA
Monee, IL
22 August 2023